INVESTIGATING
HISTORY MYSTERIES

Heinemann
LIBRARY

. . . . ALEX WOOLF . . . .

www.heinemann.co.uk/library

Visit our website to find out more information about Heinemann Library books.

To order:

☎ Phone 44 (0) 1865 888066

▤ Send a fax to 44 (0) 1865 314091

▢ Visit the Heinemann Bookshop at www.heinemann.co.uk/library to browse our catalogue and order online.

First published in Great Britain by Heinemann Library, Halley Court, Jordan Hill, Oxford OX2 8EJ, part of Harcourt Education. Heinemann is a registered trademark of Harcourt Education Ltd.

Editorial: Sarah Eason, Georga Godwin and Kate Bellamy
Design: Jo Hinton-Malivoire and AMR
Picture Research: Rosie Garai and Andrea Sadler
Production: Edward Moore

Originated by Ambassador Litho Ltd
Printed and bound in China by South China Printing Company
The paper used to print this book comes from sustainable resources

ISBN 0 431 16022 8
08 07 06 05 04
10 9 8 7 6 5 4 3 2 1

British Library Cataloguing in Publication Data
Woolf, Alex
Investigating History Mysteries
001.9'4
A full catalogue record for this book is available from the British Library.

Acknowledgements
The Publishers would like to thank the following for permission to reproduce photographs: Bridgeman/Peabody and Essex Museum p. **40**; CM Dixon pp. **8**, **16**; Corbis/Bettmann pp. **30**, **42**; Corbis pp. **6**, **20** (Ted Spiegel), **14** (David Samuel Robbins); Corbis/Ecoscene p. **41** (Andrew Brown); Graham Turner p. **34**; Greenland Museum p. **38**; Oxbow Books pp. **35**, **36**, **37**; Panos p. **7** (Paul Smith); Barrie Schwortz pp. **26**, **28**, **29**; Science Photo Library pp. **9** (James King-Holmes), **15** (John Heseltine), **18** (Robert Longuehaye) NIBSC, **31** (Martyn F Chillmaid), **33** (University of Salford Industrial Centre/ A Sternberg), **39** (Alexander Tsiaras); The National Museum of Denmark pp. **21**, **22**, **24**; Topham pp. **10**, **12**; University of Arizona p. **32** (Lori Stiles); Weezle p. **4**.

Cover photograph of the Tollund Man reproduced with permission of Science Photo Library/Silkeborg Museum, Denmark/Munoz-Yague.

The Publishers would like to thank Peter Bull and Nicola Greene for assistance in the preparation of this book.

Contents

Any words appearing in the text in bold, **like this**, are explained in the Glossary.

What is forensic science?

In its traditional sense, **forensic** science is any science used in a criminal **investigation** in order to provide evidence for use in a court of law. However, in recent times the term has been broadened to include the use of scientific techniques in historical investigations, particularly in the field of **archaeology**. Forensic science draws on a number of different disciplines, including chemistry, biology, geology and computing.

What do forensic scientists do?

Forensic scientists who work on historical mysteries employ many of the same techniques as those who assist on criminal investigations. But instead of examining the bodies of murder victims or weapons, they analyse the evidence of historical objects – clothing, jewellery, swords and helmets or human bones – and apply scientific tests to them in order to find out more about how people lived in the past. These tests can help them answer such questions as:

- how old is this object?
- what were the rites and customs of these people?
- how did this person die?

Ice-core sampling is used to research past climates by examining a tube of polar ice.

Investigating historical mysteries

There are many gaps in our knowledge of the past, from how the Pyramids were built to the identity of Jack the Ripper. Not all these mysteries can be solved through present-day science, but many can be. The case studies in this book include the stories of some of the most famous historical mysteries, and how science helped to shed light on them.

Tools to investigate the past

A whole range of scientific techniques is used to investigate historical mysteries.

Dating techniques: methods used depend on the type of object. These include **radiocarbon dating** for **organic** remains; **fluorine testing** for bones; **dendrochronology** and **ice-core sampling** for dating changes in climate and **thermoluminescence** for dating rocks and minerals.

Examining bodies: bodies or parts of bodies can be examined to find out about who they were, and how they lived and died. For example, ears can tell you a great deal about a person's health, as can teeth. Teeth can even provide information about the weather when their owners were alive. CAT scans reveal the insides of bodies, while **DNA** testing can inform you of someone's gender and physical characteristics. It is even possible to reconstruct the face of an ancestor from their skull.

Examining objects: objects can be subjected to physical and chemical tests to determine their age and origin. The ink on an old manuscript, for example, can be analysed by a process called particle induced **X-ray** emission or **Raman microprobe spectroscopy**. Even pollen grains found in the dust covering an old object can be examined for clues about what part of the world it originated from, using forensic palynology.

Clues from the past

'Stop!' shouts one of the workmen. The man working the **hydraulic excavator** stops the giant shovel just as it is about to plunge back into the earth. The workman is pointing to a small, brownish-grey object that is sticking out of the side of the pit, about 3 metres down. Though it is old and partially covered by soil, it is instantly recognizable as a human skull. The foreman orders work on the bypass to stop, and calls the local police.

Human remains

The police arrive quickly, and cordon off the pit. The inspector takes a look at the pit and shakes his head. This doesn't look like a recent burial. The skull is very old and worn. The earth above it has not been disturbed in recent times. The county council is informed, and later that day the council's heritage unit arrives, with an **osteologist** from the local university, to inspect the find. The osteologist examines the skull. His hunch is that it is very old, possibly dating back over five hundred years.

A race against time

A team of forensic **archaeologists** arrive. The construction of the bypass cannot be delayed for long, so the archaeologists must work fast. The skull is photographed and sketched. They then try to locate the rest of the skeleton. As they start digging down around the skull, they **exhume** several complete skeletons. By the day's end, they have uncovered remains of approximately twenty people, both adults and children.

The site cannot be preserved, so each skeleton must be carefully removed and taken to the university for study.

Who were these people, and how did they die? Work on a new history mystery is about

Ancient graves come in many different shapes and sizes. It's up to forensic archaeologists to find out who was buried there, and when.

Scene of an archaeological discovery

What procedures are followed to ensure historical evidence is preserved?

- Secure the scene: rope off the scene to prevent anyone from stealing or tampering with the evidence. Establish one path to and from the protected area.

- Document the scene: take photographs and make video recordings and sketches of the scene, both at the time of discovery, and as it is excavated.

- Date and identify the remains: develop a theory of what the site is and from which period of history (for example, an Anglo-Saxon burial site) based on the evidence.

- Collect evidence: do not pick up objects straight away. Flag them and photograph them first in the position they have been found, then collect them carefully and give each object an evidence number, before sealing in plastic bags and moving them to the laboratory.

A forensic anthropologist examines some human remains. Bones provide information about past peoples, their beliefs and rituals, diet and health.

Archaeological forensic science

From hand trowels to DNA fingerprinting

The application of **forensic** science to **archaeology** dates back to the 19th century, when **archaeologists** began to impose a system on the study of past objects. In 1819, a Danish archaeologist called Christian Thomsen developed a new way of classifying (putting into groups) archaeological finds. He noted that over time ancient peoples had graduated from using stone tools and weapons to bronze, before finally discovering iron. His 'Three Age System' (Stone Age, Bronze Age and Iron Age) laid the foundations for archaeology and **palaeontology**.

These flint tools date from the Stone Age, the earliest period of human history.

Layers of time

In the 1830s, the geologist Charles Lyell suggested that a section cut vertically through the earth could be divided into layers, or 'strata', with the oldest at the bottom and the most recent at the top. Any **artefacts** or remains found in a particular 'stratum' could be dated according to the layer in which they were found. Stratigraphic excavation, as Lyell's principle is known, remains a basic part of archaeology.

New principles

Between about 1860 and 1900, various methods of scientific archaeology gradually became established, including the use of field notes, photography and sketching to record excavations, and the publication of results. Archaeology became more about the discovery of how people lived, rather than simply the finding of artefacts.

The dating game

From the mid-20th century, dating of **organic** objects became more precise with the development of **radiocarbon dating**. This was followed in around 1960 by **thermoluminescence** dating, which is based on the fact that **electrons** in minerals give off light when heated. Another technique introduced in 1960 was **obsidian hydration dating**. This dates obsidian, a type of stone used as a tool in prehistoric times, by measuring the depth of the 'hydration rind', a water-rich layer on the stone's surface. Further dating techniques allow ever more precise estimates of the age of artefacts.

Archaeology today

Today, new scientific techniques and discoveries continue to affect the way archaeologists work. The arrival of **DNA** typing (see page 18) made it possible to identify the relationships between our ancestors. And techniques, such as GPS (Global Positioning System) tracking and **ground penetration radar**, have helped in the discovery and mapping of new archaeological sites.

Radiocarbon dating

Early archaeologists had no certain way of dating ancient objects. Instead, they used 'relative dating' techniques, comparing artefacts to work out which was older.

The first system of absolute dating – giving archaeologists the actual date of an object – was radiocarbon dating, developed by the American chemist, Willard Frank Libby (1908–80) in 1946.

Radiocarbon dating is based on the fact that all living things contain **carbon**, of which there are both stable and **radioactive** forms.

Carbon-14 is the radioactive form. Libby discovered that as time passes, the carbon-14 in dead organic objects decays (rots) at a given rate that can be carefully measured, so that an exact age can be determined.

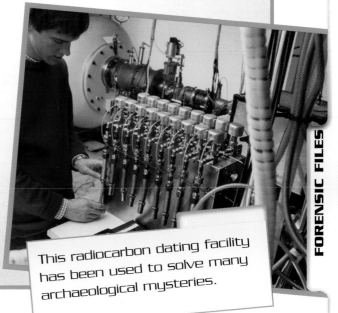

This radiocarbon dating facility has been used to solve many archaeological mysteries.

In December 1912, Charles Dawson, a solicitor and amateur **archaeologist**, made an announcement that rocked the world of **palaeontology**. He had discovered a very unusual skull in a gravel pit near Piltdown in Sussex, England. The skull had a large brain pan and an ape-like jaw, and was found in a deposit that dated from the Pliocene period (2 to 5 million years ago). This find seemed to confirm an **evolutionary** theory, popular at the time, that humans had been a race of ape-like creatures that had developed larger brains. 'Piltdown Man' was held up as a key find in the study of human evolution – the missing link between human beings and our ape-like ancestors.

Official recognition

British palaeontologists were delighted that the earliest-known ancestor of modern humans should be found in their own country, and eagerly defended the idea of Piltdown Man. French and American scientists were more doubtful at first. But the announcement in 1917 of another, similar find was enough to convert almost everyone. Dawson, who died in 1916, had found fragments of a similar skull on the same site in 1915. One skull might have been regarded as a strange find and perhaps not authentic, but two appeared to prove that Piltdown Man was genuine. The skull was given a scientific name, *Eoanthropus dawsoni*, meaning 'Dawson's Dawn Man', and entered the scientific textbooks.

Charles Dawson and Martin Hinton at the gravel pit where Dawson claimed to have found the skull.

However, in other parts of the world, evidence was being uncovered suggesting a different pattern of evolution. The discovery of the 'Taung Child' in South Africa in 1924 showed that early humans walked on two legs, but had small brains, roughly the same size as modern chimpanzees. In the 1920s and 1930s the remains of up to forty more individuals were found from a time more recent than that of Piltdown Man, and with jaws much more human-like than Piltdown, yet with smaller brains.

Many palaeontologists, such as the British anatomist Sir Arthur Keith, rejected the claims of these discoveries and others that did not fit the evolutionary pattern suggested by Piltdown Man. But as time went on, new finds continued to provide evidence for small-brained bipeds (creatures that walk on two legs), contradicting the Piltdown finds.

Testing the specimen

In 1949, a fluorine test was carried out on the Piltdown skull to find out exactly how old it was. The test proved conclusively that the skull was not from the Pliocene period, and was probably no more than about six hundred years old.

Fluorine testing

Around 1939, the palaeontologist Kenneth Oakley developed a dating technique called **fluorine testing**. Fluorine is an element found in most ground water world-wide, and can be used in a relative dating technique.

As it lies in the ground, a bone gradually absorbs fluorine from the surrounding soil and water. This causes a change in the mineral composition of the bone as it absorbs fluoride **ions** (electrically charged atoms) contained in the fluorine. The rate of this change varies according to the type of soil in the area where the bone is found. Fluorine testing is used mainly to test whether bones found in the same site were buried at the same time.

A hoax?

The first person to suggest openly that the Piltdown skull might be a hoax was a palaeontologist called J. S. Weiner, at a conference in 1953. The skull was re-examined by Weiner and two other scientists, and they quickly realized that it was a fake. The teeth on the ape-like jaw had been filed down to flatten them in order to fit the teeth of the upper jaw. The two parts of the skull were found to come from different species: the jawbone from a 500-year-old orang-utan, and the cranium (upper part of the skull) from a **medieval** human. To make the Piltdown finds look ancient the bones had been stained in an iron solution, and the canine tooth on the original skull had been painted brown!

For over forty years, the evidence of the forgery had been there for anyone who cared to look. The file marks were clearly visible on the flattened teeth, as was the paint on the tooth. The hoax had succeeded mainly because Piltdown Man confirmed a theory of evolution popular at the time, and no one suspected that it might be a **forgery**.

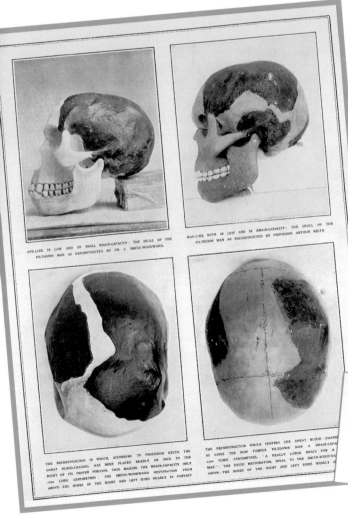

APE-LIKE IN JAW AND OF SMALL BRAIN-CAPACITY: THE SKULL OF THE PILTDOWN MAN AS RECONSTRUCTED BY DR. A. SMITH-WOODWARD.

MAN-LIKE BOTH IN JAW AND IN BRAIN-CAPACITY: THE SKULL OF THE PILTDOWN MAN AS RECONSTRUCTED BY PROFESSOR ARTHUR KEITH

THE RECONSTRUCTION IN WHICH, ACCORDING TO PROFESSOR KEITH, THE GREAT BLOOD-CHANNEL HAS BEEN PLACED NEARLY AN INCH TO THE RIGHT OF ITS PROPER POSITION. THUS MAKING THE BRAIN-CAPACITY ONLY 1070 CUBIC CENTIMETRES : THE SMITH-WOODWARD RESTORATION FROM ABOVE. THE BONES OF THE RIGHT AND LEFT SIDES NEARLY IN CONTACT.

THE RECONSTRUCTION WHICH CENTRES THE GREAT BLOOD-CHANNEL SO GIVES THE NOW FAMOUS PILTDOWN MAN A BRAIN-CAPACITY 1500 CUBIC CENTIMETRES, "A REALLY LARGE BRAIN FOR A MAN": THE KEITH RESTORATION, RIVAL TO THE SMITH-WOODWARD MAN" THE KEITH RESTORATION, RIVAL TO THE SMITH-WOODWARD ABOVE. THE BONES OF THE RIGHT AND LEFT SIDES WIDELY SE

This article printed in 1913 shows the reconstruction of Piltdown Man's skull.

Who was responsible?

After Weiner and his team proved that the Piltdown Man was a hoax, people began to wonder who was behind it and what their **motives** were. Suspicion immediately fell on Charles Dawson, the finder of the skulls. Weiner accused Dawson of the hoax in 1953. It was learned that Dawson had traded in other fake antiquities (ancient objects), which seemed to confirm that he was indeed the hoaxer. His motive is unclear, since he did not make any money out of the forgery. It is more likely that he did it for the glory of discovering a find of major scientific interest.

Did Dawson act alone?

To this day, people continue to wonder whether Dawson acted alone or had an accomplice, or whether the forger was someone else entirely. Candidates include Sir Arthur Conan Doyle, author of the Sherlock Holmes stories. He was a neighbour of Dawson's and an amateur bone hunter. One of his books, *The Lost World*, describes a similar hoax. Other than this, however, there is no hard evidence connecting Doyle to the Piltdown forgery.

A more likely hoaxer was Sir Arthur Keith, who wrote an article in 1912, before the discovery was announced, giving exact details of the location of the site. It is not clear how Keith obtained this information. According to recent research, Keith met with Dawson three times during 1911 and 1912, and later — rather suspiciously — destroyed all his correspondence (letters) with Dawson.

Another candidate was Sir Arthur Smith Woodward, keeper of the British Museum's Natural History Department. He had assisted Dawson in his excavations at Piltdown. Woodward's involvement in the hoax would explain why tests initially carried out on the skull did not expose the forgery, for Woodward was careful about who saw the find.

In early 2001, two scientists from the University of Hong Kong, David Zhang and S. H. Li, were on a mountain slope high up in the Tibetan plateau, some 53 miles (85 kilometres) from the Tibetan capital, Lhasa. Near a hot spring, they came across an unexpected find: human handprints and footprints embedded in the marble-like rock. They also found the remains of a fireplace and primitive stove nearby. It looked like an ancient camp or settlement. Intrigued, the scientists wondered how old the prints were.

Ice Age settlers

The rock in which the prints were found was a hard limestone called travertine, which is formed when the soft mud left by a hot spring dries. The prints would have been made when it was still soft mud, so in order to date the prints, Zhang and Li needed to find out when the travertine had formed. Through a process known as **thermoluminescence** dating they were able to work out that the travertine had formed 20,000 years before.

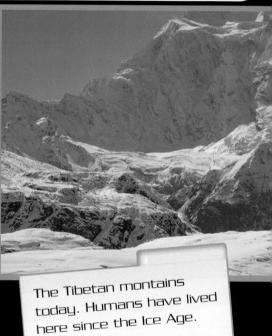

The Tibetan montains today. Humans have lived here since the Ice Age.

At a stroke, this discovery changed our knowledge of the human history of the region. Until these prints were found and dated, the oldest-known human settlements on the Tibetan plateau were around 4000 years old. It was now proved that humans had actually lived in this area 16,000 years earlier than that, during the **Ice Age** – a time when it was thought that the Tibetan plateau had been covered by a 1000 metres-thick glacier (mass of moving ice). The hand- and footprints showed that at least part

Time capsule

We will never know the story of the people who left these prints, but it is likely that the hot spring had attracted them to this area. Nineteen prints were found in all, belonging to at least six individuals, including two children. The travertine acted like a time capsule preserving forever the marks of this mysterious prehistoric group.

Thermoluminescence dating

This is a method of dating rock by measuring the amount of energy in quartz, a mineral contained within the rock.

Energy builds up within quartz when it is exposed to **radiation** from surrounding minerals. (Radiation is a form of energy emitted from certain elements, such as uranium or thorium, the atoms of which are not stable, and which spontaneously decay.) The quartz gives this energy off as light.

The longer the quartz is exposed to radiation, the greater the energy and the brighter the light. The energy of the quartz is released by heat or sunlight, so when the quartz grains became embedded in the warm mud from the spring, the energy would have been zero. It was therefore an easy calculation to work out when the mud hardened into travertine.

Quartz can glow after exposure to radiation. This is called thermoluminescence.

Human sacrifice

The ancient Phoenicians were a highly cultured, seagoing people, who developed from around 3000 BC to 64 BC. Phoenicia was based in present-day Lebanon, Syria and Israel. From the 9th century BC they settled in many parts of the eastern Mediterranean, including Carthage in North Africa, Cyprus and Sicily. As part of the worship of their god Baal, the Phoenicians regularly sacrificed animals. According to accounts by their enemies, the Romans, the Phoenicians also sacrificed their children.

Discovering the remains

In the 1970s **archaeological** excavations at the Phoenician city of Carthage in North Africa revealed a sacred area, known as a Tophet, where sacrifices may have been carried out. Beneath some standing stones, **archaeologists** found about 20,000 clay urns (special containers for human ashes). These contained the burnt remains of human infants. For those experts who believed the Roman accounts, this appeared to be conclusive evidence that child sacrifice did take place. One historian, Professor Bartoloni, a specialist in Phoenician history, was not convinced. He believed the Tophet was actually a cemetery for stillborn babies, or those who died soon after birth.

Headstones of children's graves at the Carthage Tophet. Was this a place of burial or sacrifice?

Early in the summer of 2000, archaeologists excavated another Tophet in the Phoenician city of Motya, near Sicily, where they uncovered 6000 more urns also filled with human bones. Over a three-month period, scientists in Britain and Israel used the latest **forensic** techniques to analyse the remains found in the urns of Carthage and Motya to try to solve the mystery: did the Phoenicians really sacrifice their children, or was the Tophet simply a burial ground for Phoenician infants?

Analysing the bones

It was the task of Dr Charlotte Roberts, a biological **anthropologist**, to analyse bones from the Motya urns for clues to the state of health of the children before they died. If they showed signs of disease, then the chances were that this was a cemetery. If they were healthy, then it would indicate that they had been sacrificed.

Despite the great age and damaged state of the bones, Dr Roberts was able to determine that the bones did indeed belong to infants, although these were mixed up with bones from sheep, goats and birds. Supporters of the 'sacrifice' theory pointed to this as evidence that both animals and children were sacrificed at the same ceremonies. Bartoloni, however, pointed out that it was common practice for a child's body to be accompanied by the body of an animal for companionship on the journey to the next life.

Teeth analysis

Charlotte Roberts also discovered human teeth among the remains. Teeth are a strong indicator of general health, and can show signs of disorders such as rickets (soft, bendy bones), anaemia (lack of red blood cells) or vitamin deficiencies.

After examining samples of tooth enamel from 20 children under a microscope, she concluded that they did not suffer from disease or any nutritional problems.

So far all the evidence was pointing to the same conclusion: the children had been sacrificed. To settle the matter, it was necessary to identify the sex of the children. According to contemporary accounts, it was the custom that only male infants were sacrificed, so it would be logical to find only the remains of boys at the Carthage and Motya Tophets.

Extracting the DNA

It was decided that the best way of determining the gender of the children would be to extract **DNA** from the bone samples. DNA is a kind of **molecule** found in the cells of all living creatures. DNA is the major component of **genes** – that carry information about the creature – including its physical characteristics, and its gender.

British microbiologists (scientists who study microscopic organisms) Ron Dixon and Keri Brown were chosen to extract the DNA. All genes – including those that determine gender – are formed into structures called **chromosomes**. Males have an X and a Y chromosome, while females have two X chromosomes. Therefore, if Dixon and Brown found DNA from a Y chromosome, they would know it had come from a male infant.

DNA that was extracted from old bones is cloned (copied) so there is enough to study.

teeth and bone samples were taken to their laboratory in England.
The samples were put through cycles of heating and cooling, alongside a
substance called polymerase, which magnified the tiny fragments of DNA
until they were big enough to be analysed. The samples were then stained
in a special gel and viewed under **ultraviolet** light to see if any DNA was
present. If two bands were visible, it would indicate a male; one band
would indicate a female. Twelve attempts proved fruitless. Then, on the
thirteenth attempt, they succeeded. When they looked at the gel, they
saw a solitary band of DNA – it was a girl!

Conclusion

This discovery was a setback for supporters of the child sacrifice theory.
However, more work was needed before the question could be resolved.
In 2000 the Israeli team embarked on a five-year study of 2000 infants
from the Carthage Tophet. The work of Dixon and Brown had at least
proved that DNA could be extracted from 3000-year-old cremated bones.

DNA typing

Dixon and Brown were simply trying to work out
gender from the extracted DNA. However, in cases
where remains are better preserved or less ancient,
and the DNA is easier to obtain, scientists can use
it to find out a lot more about someone's identity
and physical characteristics, and their
relationships to others.

Although large parts of our DNA are identical
(because each of us has the same organs and body
parts), other sections of our DNA vary from person
to person. By studying these varying segments,
scientists can work out whether a strand of DNA
came from a particular individual.

DNA can be extracted from blood, soft tissue, even
hair and fingernail clippings — as well as bones.

The Vikings that vanished

In the year of 1340, a Norwegian sailor named Ivar Bardarson paid a visit to a colony of Vikings living on the west coast of Greenland. What he found there was truly shocking. The entire settlement – which just a few years before had been a thriving community of farms, schools and churches – was completely deserted. Bardarson reported: 'I saw nobody, neither Christians nor Heathens, only some wild cattle and sheep, all running wild.'

The Norse colonies on Greenland

The Vikings, from present-day Scandinavia, first settled on Greenland when Erik the Red sailed there in 982. By the year 1000 there were about 1000 settlers. At its height, the colony probably contained around 6000 people, divided among three communities, known as the Eastern, Middle and Western Settlements.

Viking ruins of one of the deserted settlements in Greenland.

For some reason, the Western Settlement vanished almost overnight in 1340. The remaining two settlements disappeared with similar suddenness 160 years later, and by 1500 there were no Vikings left in Greenland. Different theories have been put forward to explain the disappearances. It has been suggested that they were victims of the plague that ravaged Europe during the 14th century, or that they perished in a war with the native Inuit. But it wasn't until the 20th century that serious attempts were made to solve the mystery of the vanished Vikings.

Studying the bones

In the early 20th century, graves from the settlements were excavated, and the remains of around 350 individuals removed. In 1924 a Norwegian **archaeologist**, F.C.C. Hansen, examined 27 of these skeletons. He noted that many of them were small and slightly built, some showing signs of a bone disease called rickets. 'The tall northern race,' Hansen wrote, 'has thus degenerated into small, slight and delicate women, and correspondingly slightly taller men, a striking example of the well-known effect of chronic under-nourishment and hard conditions of life.'

Dr Niels Lynnerup from the University of Copenhagen, Denmark carried out further forensic tests on excavated bones in the 1980s. Dr Lynnerup noticed that there was more middle-ear disease in the 14th and 15th centuries than in earlier times. This discovery pointed to a dramatic decline in the health of the settlers by the later period.

Dr Lynnerup also noticed high numbers of young women among the dead. The deaths of so many women of childbearing age could endanger a small, isolated community, whose survival depended on the supply of new babies.

Ear analysis

The study of ears can provide a good picture of the general health of a community. This is because the ear, owing to its delicate construction, is particularly prone to disease.

Middle-ear infection, also known as acute otitis media, is often found in areas where the people are poorly nourished. This inflammation of the middle ear can be caused by an allergic reaction, a virus or bacteria and — if not treated with medicine — can lead to meningitis (infection in the brain), facial paralysis or a brain abscess.

These are the remains of a bishop who was unearthed near the Viking cathedral in the Eastern settlement.

Starvation

It was looking likely that inadequate diet may have been a factor in the disappearances. Further evidence suggested that something even worse had occurred. In the kitchen of a ruined farmhouse, partly buried in **silt**, archaeologists found the bones of a Norwegian elkhound – a Viking hunting dog. The bones were knife-marked, proving the dog had been eaten. It is unlikely that a Viking would have killed and eaten his hunting dog unless he and his family had been starving.

Fly spotting

Famine conditions at the silted-over farmhouse were confirmed by an analysis by Dr Peter Skidmore of Sheffield University, UK, of fossilized flies found there. Skidmore discovered fossils of a warmth-loving species of fly on the floors of the farmhouse living room and bedroom – exactly where one would expect to find them. Another kind of fly, favouring colder conditions and living on meat, was found – also as expected – in the food store. However, in the top layer of silt, formed in the final days of the Viking settlement, Skidmore noticed that the warmth-loving flies had gone, and the cold-loving meat-eaters had moved from the larder to the bedroom. They had come to feed on the dead bodies of the settlers.

This gravestone marked one of the graves found at the Viking colony.

In an effort to understand how this famine could have occurred, archaeologists contacted researchers on the Greenland Ice Sheet Project. These researchers were using a method called **ice-core sampling** to study changes in the regional **climate**. The ice-cores extracted in Greenland showed that when the Vikings arrived in around the year 1000, the climate was quite mild – even better than it was in Scandinavia at the time. But further tests showed that during the later period of the settlement the weather grew far colder; in fact, a mini-ice age had hit Greenland at this time. The freezing weather killed the livestock and seedlings, which caused a famine.

Ice-core sampling

This method involves drilling down through the ice sheet with a hollow drill and extracting a long tube of ice, about five inches in diameter, known as a core. This provides researchers with a record of average temperatures over thousands of years. Since air temperature controls the amount of oxygen or hydrogen in snow, scientists can measure the amounts of these elements at any point in the ice core, and from this work out the average temperature at a particular period of history.

As well as looking at oxygen and hydrogen levels, ice-core samplers can also measure levels of deuterium, which is a kind of heavy water **molecule**. In warm weather, deuterium evaporates readily into the atmosphere to fall later as snow. But when the temperature drops, deuterium resists evaporation, because it is slightly heavier than water, and less of it reaches the atmosphere. High deuterium levels in the ice core indicate warm temperatures. However, studies of the ice-core in the area of the Viking settlements showed unusually low levels of deuterium at the end of the community's history. This indicated that the climate had become significantly colder.

Every tooth tells a tale

In 1994, Henry Fricke, a graduate student at the University of Michigan, USA, carried out a study on the teeth of Viking settlers. He believed that the settlers' teeth contained an accurate record of the temperatures in their lifetime. This is because the Vikings obtained their drinking water from local water supplies, such as springs, lakes and rivers. The oxygen in this water would be incorporated into their bodies and blood, and eventually their teeth.

By analysing the oxygen isotopes (atoms with differing numbers of neutrons) in the teeth, Fricke could obtain a record of the changes in temperature at the time these people were living. The **ratio** of heavy oxygen isotopes (oxygen atoms with 9 neutrons) to light oxygen isotopes (containing 8 neutrons) in the enamel of their teeth would give him the ratio of oxygen isotopes in the rain and snow from the time they were living. Local temperatures in turn, control the oxygen isotope ratio of rain and snowfall. Therefore, by analysing the oxygen isotope ratio in teeth, Fricke was able to learn about the temperatures in the area.

Analysis of the tooth enamel of these teeth told scientists what the temperature was like when the person was alive.

Fricke's experiments confirmed the results of the ice-core sampling. They showed a dramatic drop in temperature on Greenland in the middle of the 14th century, around the time when the Western Settlement disappeared. The miniature ice age experienced at that time would have been devastating for the Viking colonies, causing their crops to fail and leaving their livestock without food for the winter.

Beetle studies

Evidence of failed harvests came in a study of beetle fossils found on the Viking farms. Beetles would have lived in the fields and haylofts of the settlements, but it was clear from counting the fossils that the beetle numbers decreased sharply from the mid-14th century onwards. The Vikings could have adapted – like the native Inuit – to the harsher climate by abandoning farming and turning to hunting and fishing. However, it is thought likely that their Christian beliefs deterred them from associating with the non-Christian Inuit, so they were unable to learn from them.

Conclusion

Instead, it appears that the Viking communities in Greenland suffered a bleak and painful end, succumbing to ear infections and other illnesses, weakened by malnutrition and slaughtering their hunting dogs for food.

Analysing the teeth

For his tests Fricke needed only a few grains of tooth enamel, which he obtained from the surface of each tooth with a hand drill fitted with a dentist's burr (file). To extract the oxygen from the enamel, the samples were first dissolved in hydrofluoric acid. Silver nitrate solution was then added to the solution, which was heated, to produce a silver phosphate. A few particles of graphite were added to the mixture, which was then heated to 1400°C.

The silver phosphate reacted with the graphite to form carbon dioxide. The carbon dioxide was then analysed by a process called **accelerator mass spectrometry**, which uses magnetic and electrical fields to separate the components (parts) of a gas. These are then identified and counted.

At 5 a.m. on 21 April 1988, the archbishop of Turin, in Italy, stood in the Royal Chapel of the city's cathedral watching the priest slowly, carefully removing the holy Shroud from its casket. Later, the archbishop met with a group of scientists from the Shroud of Turin Research Project (STURP) that had been requesting permission to **radiocarbon date** the shroud. A lengthy discussion followed about where on the Shroud the sample should be taken from. Then, at 9:45, a video camera recorded the event as a tiny piece was cut from one edge of the Shroud and was divided into three pieces. The pieces were then wrapped in foil, placed in sealed canisters and taken away for testing.

What is it?

The Turin Shroud is a piece of linen cloth, bearing the image of a bearded man. For centuries, many believed – and continue to believe – that this was the Shroud in which Jesus Christ was buried after he was crucified, and that miraculously the image of his body had become imprinted on the cloth. Hand wounds, like those said to have been suffered by Jesus at his crucifixion, are visible.

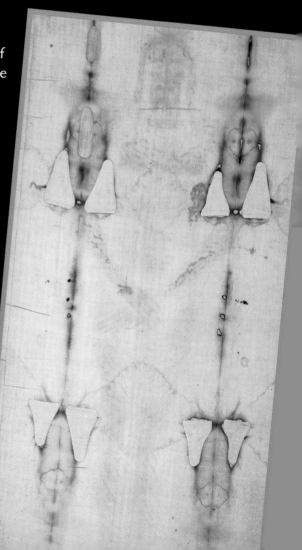

The Turin Shroud is the most studied object in history. Yet there is still no agreement about its origins.

The first recorded mention of the Shroud of Turin was in 1317. It was then in the possession of a French knight called Geoffrey de Charny, who was said to have acquired it in Constantinople. In 1532, it narrowly escaped destruction in a fire, in Sainte Chapelle, Chambéry, and in 1578 it reached Turin, by way of Jerusalem, Odessa and Constantinople.

Dating the shroud

The idea of radiocarbon dating the Shroud was first proposed in 1978, but it was ten years before the plan was finally put into action. Scientists from STURP, representing three laboratories – in Oxford (UK), Arizona (USA) and Zurich (Switzerland) – were chosen to do the dating.

In October 1988, the results of the radiocarbon dating were announced. The linen of the Shroud had almost certainly been manufactured between 1260 and 1390 AD – many centuries after Jesus died. Around the world, newspaper headlines declared the Shroud a fake. The Catholic Church accepted the findings.

Accelerator mass spectrometry

The radiocarbon dating of the Shroud was made possible thanks to the development in 1977 of a new technique called **accelerator mass spectrometry** (AMS), pioneered by Professor Harry Gove of Rochester University, New York.

In radiocarbon dating, scientists measure the amount of **carbon-14** in an object, and thereby calculate its age (see page 9). AMS uses a **particle accelerator** in conjunction with large magnets and gas ionization detectors, which count the ions one at a time as they come down the beamline, to separate out the atoms of carbon-14 in order to count them.

Carbon is first extracted from the sample, and then the particle accelerator produces a beam of carbon ions (carbon atoms with an electric charge) from the sample. A magnet is used to reject the stable carbon, and select the **radioactive** carbon-14 atoms, which can then be counted by a device called a gas ionization detector.

The first photograph

Although revered by Christians for centuries, it was not until 1898 that the Shroud became a legend. At a public exhibition in that year, an Italian amateur photographer took the first ever photograph of the Shroud. When the negative of that photograph was published, clearly showing the image of a man many thought to be Jesus, it brought the Shroud to the attention of the world.

Studying the pollen

Over the next seven decades, there was much debate about the authenticity of the Shroud, but no direct testing. Then, in November 1973, it was secretly examined by a team of experts, including Dr Max Frei, a Swiss criminologist (someone who studies crime). Frei was a specialist in a field known as **forensic** palynology – the study of pollen for forensic purposes. He used adhesive tape to lift samples of dust from the surface of the Shroud. Pollen grains found in this dust were found to come from plants commonly found in Israel and the surrounding area. So, even if the Turin Shroud was a **medieval** fake, it came from the right part of the world.

The image of a man

In 1978, a further study was carried out on the Shroud. Scientists subjected samples to various forms of chemical and physical analysis. The Shroud had been in contact with a body, which

Dr Max Frei uses adhesive tape to lift off dust, pollen and other matter from the fibres of the Shroud.

explained the scourge (whip) marks and the blood (which was genuine). The scientists believed the image was produced by some process that caused the oxidation (addition of oxygen) and dehydration (removal of water) of the structure of the microfibrils (microscopic threads) that made up the linen. But this did not explain how the image of a man had become imprinted on the cloth.

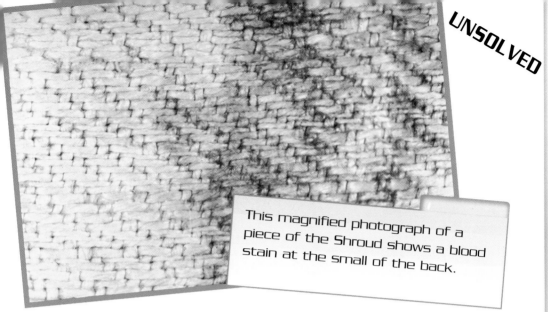

This magnified photograph of a piece of the Shroud shows a blood stain at the small of the back.

Unanswered questions

In recent years, doubts have been cast on the results of the 1988 radiocarbon dating tests. Some claim the samples were taken from an area of the cloth that had been stitched on in the Middle Ages. Others, that bacteria had built up over the centuries on the surface of the linen and confused the dating process. The official view remains that the Shroud is a medieval production. However, the mystery of the Turin Shroud is likely to go on being debated for many years to come.

Forensic palynology

The study of pollen — or palynology — is being used increasingly for forensic purposes. For example, pollen found in soil samples taken from the bottom of a suspect's shoes can be matched to the pollen at the scene of a crime.

Each type of plant produces a unique 'pollen fingerprint', which includes its durability, physical shape, weight, method and distance of dispersal, quantity and 'sinking speed' (the rate at which it falls to earth). The task of the forensic palynologist is to match the pollen in a known geographical region with the pollen in a forensic sample.

FILE CLOSED

Lawrence Witten was a rare-book dealer in New Haven, Connecticut, USA. In 1957, a volume was offered to him containing a map, supposedly dating from around 1440. The map showed Europe and Greenland, and to the left, an area labelled Vinland – the name given to a part of North America supposedly discovered by the Viking explorer Leif Eriksson around the year 1000. If genuine, this would be the oldest-known map of North America in existence. It would also prove that the American continent was known to Europeans 50 years before Columbus's 1492 voyage. It also provided evidence that Eriksson had reached North America well before Columbus. Witten believed in the map's authenticity and he paid the anonymous seller $3500 for it.

Various artists have imagined how Leif Eriksson might have discovered North America. In this painting Eriksson directs his sailors towards the coast of Vinland.

Wormholes

Witten showed the book to scholars at Yale University. They noticed that the bindings of the volume containing the map were relatively recent, and that the **medieval** manuscript – entitled the *Tartar Relation* – bound alongside the map had holes made by bookworms that did not match the wormholes in the map. It was as if they had been produced at different places and times, and simply bound into one volume.

Then, in 1958, Witten came across a medieval encyclopaedia called *Speculum Historiale*. By an amazing chance, he found that the wormholes on the last page of the encyclopaedia matched those on the first page of the *Tartar Relation*, and that the wormholes on the first page of the encyclopaedia matched those on the map. They had obviously all once been part of the same volume. Since the *Speculum Historiale* was a well-known, and undoubtedly genuine work, from the mid-15th century it seemed that the map was in fact authentic.

The yellow pigment

In 1965, the 'Vinland Map' as it became known, was acquired by the Beinecke Library at Yale University. And for several years the document took pride of place as the greatest treasure of the Yale map collection. Then, in 1972, in order to remove any lingering doubts about the map, Yale offered it to an independent laboratory for tests. **Forensic** scientist Walter McCrone's microscopic analysis of the ink showed that it contained a yellow **pigment** called anatase, a form of titanium oxide rare in nature. It was not commercially available until after 1923. The university was forced to admit that the map 'may be a **forgery**'.

Then, in 1985, a further analysis, using more sophisticated techniques, cast doubt on McCrone's findings. **Physicists** from the University of California at Davis, led by Thomas Cahill, were able to show that the ink contained only the smallest traces of anatase – consistent with the amounts found in other medieval documents.

Paper chromatography reveals the composition of ink by separating the chemicals that make it up. This chromatogram shows the composition of black ink.

The debate continues

The findings did not convince McCrone, who claimed that the crystal form of the anatase could not have been found in nature. Cahill argued that the crystals were a result of modern **contamination** rather than modern forgery. Over the years, the arguments between the supporters of the map and those who regarded it as a fake grew increasingly heated, with neither side seemingly able to prove their case conclusively.

New tests

In 2002, two new tests were carried out. The first was a **radiocarbon dating** test on the **parchment**, carried out at Brookhaven National Laboratory in Upton, New York. The test established that the parchment was 15th century, and was made sometime between 1423 and 1445. This did not change the views of those who thought it a forgery, as the parchment may have been much older than the ink used for the map.

Two chemists at University College London, Robin Clark and Katherine Brown, carried out a second test. They used a technique called **Raman microprobe spectroscopy** to identify the composition of the ink. The results showed that anatase was present on the lines alone and not elsewhere on the map. This disproved Cahill's theory that the crystals were caused by modern contamination. If that had been the case, anatase would have been found all over the map's surface, not just in the ink.

The samples of parchment from the Vinland Map were found to date from the 15th century – before Columbus's journey.

The debate rumbles on. One way to settle the issue might be to radiocarbon date the ink. However, current dating techniques would require a lot more ink than can be provided by the map.

Thomas Cahill thinks the mystery of the Vinland Map will never be solved. 'It'll never be settled,' he says. 'There are a million ways to prove something fraudulent [dishonest], and no way to prove it is genuine.'

Raman microprobe spectroscopy

The basis of this technique is that when light rays of a particular frequency strike the **molecules** of a substance such as ink, most of the scattered rays continue at the same frequency, but a few are scattered at a variety of changed frequencies. These are known collectively as a Raman spectrum, which gives a very precise indication of what a substance is made of. The Raman microprobe spectroscope (RMS) is an instrument that can show the Raman spectrum of a substance, to work out its chemical composition.

Clark and Brown used the RMS to work out what the Vinland Map's ink was made of. They found that the map's lines were made of two different substances: their black centres were **carbon**, and their yellowish edges contained anatase. Black lines with yellowish edges are often found in manuscripts written with iron gall ink, popular since the Middle Ages. Iron gall ink is made from plant tannins and iron sulphate, but Brown and Clark did not find these substances in the map's ink. They concluded that a forger had attempted to mimic the look of iron gall ink by using a carbon-based ink and adding the yellow anatase.

A laser beam projected at an ink sample will cause a Raman spectrum to form, which will show what chemicals the ink is made from.

Medieval warfare: myth and reality

In August 1996, during the construction of an extension at Towton Hall in Yorkshire, England, workmen uncovered a burial pit containing several human skeletons. A team of **forensic archaeologists** and bone specialists from Bradford University was summoned, and began the work of exhuming the skeletons. They were found to have belonged to soldiers who had died in the 15th-century conflicts known as the Wars of the Roses.

The Wars of the Roses were a series of civil wars fought from 1455 to 1485, between the families of York and Lancaster for the throne of England. The climax of this conflict – and the bloodiest battle – took place near the village of Towton in Yorkshire on 29 March 1461, when up to 28,000 men lost their lives. By studying the remains at Towton Hall, archaeologists hoped to learn more about **medieval** warfare, and the lives of ordinary soldiers from this period.

This painting by Graham Turner shows the battle between King Edward IV's army and the Lancastrians.

Skeleton studies

Osteologists assist in the **exhuming** of bones and the restoration of skeletons. In the laboratory, the osteologists' first task was to determine the age of the soldiers when they died. By examining their bones, they calculated that the dead ranged in age from 16 to 50.

Radiocarbon dating confirmed that the bodies dated from the Battle of Towton. The cause of their deaths was obvious from the horrific wounds on each of the skulls. One soldier had thirteen head injuries.

Longbowmen

Because there were entire skeletons, it was possible to examine the former body structure of the soldiers, and to learn something about the health of the average 15th-century fighting man. A number of them had better developed left arms than right, indicating that they may have been archers – users of the longbow.

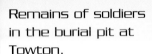
Remains of soldiers in the burial pit at Towton.

Determining age from bones

Working out the age of an individual from a skeleton calls for experience and skill. The bones of young children are easier, because various growth changes are taking place, such as development of the ends of limb bones and the emergence of teeth.

With under-25-year-olds, an estimate within two to three years can be made by measuring the joining up of epiphyses. These are small parts of bone separated from the main bone by a layer of **cartilage**.

With over-25-year-olds it is harder, as the skeleton is now mature. However, if any of the skull sutures (the lines between the bones of the head) have not completely closed, it is likely that the individual was under 30.

The longbowmen's fate

To test the theory that these were longbowmen, **anthropologist** Chris Knusel needed to find a modern-day archer and see if he had developed similar changes in his body. He approached lifelong archer Simon Stanley, who agreed to a body scan. After careful comparison, it became clear that Simon's arms had developed in exactly the same way as the arms of the soldiers found in the burial pit.

Number sixteen

The sixteenth skeleton recovered belonged to a strong-boned man in his late forties. Number Sixteen carried a horrific injury to the left side of his jaw that had evidently healed long before Towton. The wound was so deep that it had caused a secondary fracture to his chin, and would have severely damaged his mouth and tongue. Yet amazingly he had survived, and the wound had eventually healed. Deep wounds easily become infected, and the absence of infection from this wound and others revealed the skills of medieval battlefield surgeons.

The skull of this Towton victim shows evidence of savagery.

The Bradford team wanted to know what Number Sixteen had looked like, so they asked **forensic artist** Richard Neave to use Number Sixteen's skull to make a reconstruction of his head. Neave's task was made harder by the damage Number Sixteen's skull had sustained at the time of his death, including the destruction of a large portion of the left side of his head. Nevertheless, the finished result was impressive, making him easier to imagine as a person – a mature fighting man with strong features and a rather frightening scar.

Massacre

From an analysis of the wounds on the 37 skeletons, it was found that most had died by sword, dagger or battleaxe. Only one arrow wound was found. The soldiers had clearly been attacked and killed at close quarters, almost all dying from a single, powerful blow to the head, followed by several more blows on the head and face. The wound patterns also showed that the soldiers' heads had been unprotected by helmets when the blows were struck. Only one conclusion was possible: they were prisoners who had been massacred, possibly Lancastrians – prisoners of Edward IV, a Yorkist, who defeated the enemy that day. The code of honour that may have existed between medieval knights clearly did not extend to common soldiers.

Facial reconstruction

The skull is always the starting point for facial reconstruction, as it determines the exact proportions of the face, such as the width between the eyes and the size of the nose. Neave made a copy of the skull, then used his knowledge of human anatomy to recreate the muscle groups on the skull's surface, and to build up the soft tissue to its likely depth.

The hardest part was reconstructing the unknown aspects, such as the tip of the nose, the eyebrows and forehead creases. This required some educated guesswork, but Neave was confident that the finished result would bear a strong resemblance to the real Number Sixteen.

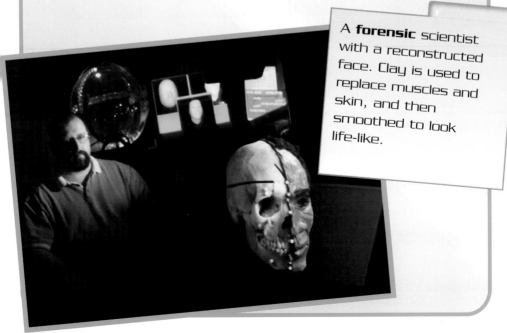

A **forensic** scientist with a reconstructed face. Clay is used to replace muscles and skin, and then smoothed to look life-like.

In October 1972, two brothers Hans and Jokum Gronvold, were on a bird-hunting expedition in a desolate area known as Qilakitsoq on the western coast of Greenland. Seeking shelter from the freezing winds in a cave, they were greeted by an astonishing sight: eight dead bodies – six women, a child and a baby – all in perfect condition. The brothers informed the authorities of their discovery, and it was not long before scientists and **archaeologists** came to **investigate**.

Freeze-dried mummies

The bodies were found to belong to a tribe of the native Inuit people. Through **radiocarbon dating** it was possible to determine that they had died in about 1475 – they had lain undiscovered in the cave for 500 years, making them the oldest preserved (in good condition) bodies in Greenland! The dry, icy conditions and cold winds had preserved their bodies and clothes so well that they had barely deteriorated (rotted).

Questions immediately arose about the discovery: how did they die? Why were there no men in the group? Inuit women and children were not normally buried separately from their men. Perhaps they were victims of a boat accident, and had drowned together?

A **forensic** archaeologist examined the bodies using a CAT scan, which gives a three-dimensional picture of the inside of the body. Food was found in the women's stomachs and intestines, so they clearly did not starve to death. Nor did they die of cold – their sealskin clothing would have protected them from the freezing conditions.

This 500-year-old mummified Inuit baby's clothes were made from the soft fur and skin of baby seals.

Buried alive

One woman was found to have a malignant tumour (an unusual mass of cells that invades the healthy cells around it) near the base of her skull, which was a likely cause of death. The older child had a disease of the hip joint that may have made him vulnerable to other life-threatening diseases. The baby, who was around six months old when he died, appeared to have been buried alive. At this time it was Inuit practice to bury babies alive if a woman could not be found to nurse them.

A picture of the past

Examination of the bodies told much about these people's lives. The adults had complicated tattoos on their skin. Soot from seal-blubber lamps coated their lungs and the food in their stomachs revealed a diet of seals and deer.

How the Inuit women died remains a mystery, but the bodies have provided valuable information about how the Inuit lived over five hundred years ago.

CAT scans

CAT (Computerized Axial Tomography) scans give a three-dimensional image of the inside of an object. **X-rays** are directed at the object from all angles to provide images of sections through it. A computer then puts these images together to create a reconstruction of the object in three dimensions.

TURN ANGLE = -10

CAT scans are used in medicine to diagnose cancer and other diseases, but they are also a tool in forensic **archaeology**.

Witches and rye

In 1692, the town of Salem in Massachusetts, USA became the scene of some strange and disturbing behaviour. Eight of the young town women fell victim to fits, outbreaks of obscene (rude) babbling, and wild partying in the local woodland. The girls blamed other members of the community, claiming they were witches who had caused them to become possessed by the devil. The accused were put on trial, and on the basis of evidence given by the afflicted girls, nineteen people were hanged for witchcraft.

No adequate explanation has ever been given for the behaviour of the girls. Some experts believe they were **motivated** by jealousy or spite, and their strange behaviour was an act. Others have put it down to hysteria, a kind of mental illness.

This painting shows the trial of George Jacobs, one of those accused of witchcraft in Salem, 1692.

Hallucinations?

In 1976, a psychologist called Linnda Caporael re-examined the case. She didn't accept the standard explanations. The symptoms were too real to be acted, and it was unlikely that eight girls would become hysterical at the same time. One night, while reading an account of the events, she came across a passage referring to the girls' **'hallucinations'**. The use of this word gave Caporael an idea. Maybe the girls had experienced a natural form of the hallucinogenic drug, Lysergic Acid Diethylamide (LSD). She knew that LSD was derived from a poisonous fungus called ergot that often grows on the grains of cereals, especially rye – a common crop in the USA at the time.

Caporael looked up the symptoms of ergot poisoning and found they included convulsive jerking, stupor, delirium (confusion) and hallucinations – precisely the symptoms displayed by the girls.

Wider implications

The historian Mary Matossian decided to see if ergot might account for other outbreaks of witchcraft in history. She studied witch trials in Europe and then looked at the rye-growing areas on the continent. The results amazed her. In every part of Europe the areas dependent on rye had a significantly higher level of witch persecution. By studying **dendrochronology** (tree ring analysis) records, Matossian was able show that in cold, wet years, when ergot grows best, the number of witchcraft trials rose. Can the persecution of witches really be explained by a plant disease? It's an intriguing possibility.

Dendrochronology

Concentric rings mark the trunks of many trees, in cross-section. Each ring represents a year in the tree's life. These rings mark the limit of growth during the tree's annual growing seasons, and the amount of growth – and the size of the ring – is affected by factors like temperature and rainfall.

Samples are taken by using a hollow drill to extract a tube of the tree's trunk from the bark to the centre. This can be compared with samples from other trees to build up a general picture of **climatic** history in a certain area.

Wide rings show a wet climate, and narrow rings show a dry climate.

Solve it!

So, you've read the book. You've seen the professionals in action. Now how do you fancy trying to solve a history mystery for yourself? Imagine that you're a **forensic archaeologist**. You must decide which of the techniques described in the book you would use to solve this case ...

The legendary king

You receive a letter from the Minister of Cultural Affairs from the tiny European republic of Principalia. He has invited you to inspect some human remains. According to local tradition they are the bones of King Maxwell I. Maxwell was a heroic figure from the country's distant past, who – if you believe the legend – withstood the invading Huns from Asia, and kept Principalia free. Maxwell reputedly died at the age of 28 at the Battle of Chalôns in 451, killed by Attila, King of the Huns. His statue can be seen in the square of every Principalian town.

The remains

The skeleton of a man believed to be Maxwell can be found in the cathedral at Principolis, the nation's capital. It is kept on permanent display in a gold and glass case in the cathedral's crypt. The skeleton lies wrapped in a very old, bloodstained woollen cloak, supposed to be the one he wore in battle. Nearby, in its own glass case, is the earliest known likeness of Maxwell – a picture of his face on a coin, supposedly made in

This painting by Alexander Zick shows Attila, King of the Huns.

his lifetime. How the remains arrived in their present location is lost in the mists of time. The first official acknowledgement of their existence came in a cathedral inventory (list) written in 1426.

Science and superstition

Every year, on 22 July, the date of Maxwell's great victory, the case is opened, and the public are allowed to kiss the hem of his cloak. Miracles are said to occur on that day. The Culture Minister explains in his letter that he is concerned at his fellow citizens' superstitious beliefs, and wishes to cast a scientific light on these ancient myths. The minister has rules for your **investigation**. You are allowed to take only the skull, one or two bones, and a tiny piece of the cloak back to your laboratory for testing. The rest must remain untouched and unexamined.

What you must do

Your task is to search for clues that could link these remains to King Maxwell. You must decide what techniques you would use to answer the following questions:

1 Do the bones of the dead man in the glass case date from the 5th century?
2 How old was the dead man when he died?
3 Did the man look like the face on the coin?
4 How old is the cloak?
5 Did the cloak belong to the dead man?
6 Did the cloak come from Principalia?

ANSWERS
1 Use **radiocarbon dating** to find the age of the bones.
2 Examine the skull to work out the age of the man. If the skull sutures are not completely closed, it would indicate that he was under 30 years old. With under-25-year-olds, an estimate can be made by measuring progress on the joining up of epiphyses, which are small parts of bone separated from the main bone by a layer of cartilage.
3 Employ a **forensic artist** to use the skull as a basis for a facial reconstruction.
4 Use **accelerator mass spectrometry** to radiocarbon date the tiny sample of the cloak.
5 Extract samples of **DNA** from the blood on the cloak and the bones, and see if they come from the same person.
6 Take a dust sample from the cloak and examine the **pollen** grains to work out where the cloak originated.

Glossary

accelerator mass spectrometry method of radiocarbon dating an object that works by separating out and counting the atoms of carbon-14

anthropologist scientist who studies human culture and development

archaeologist scientist who studies past cultures by examining their material remains

archaeology study of ancient cultures through the examination of their physical remains

artefacts object made by a human being, such as a tool or sculpture, especially one that is of interest to archaeologists

carbon non-metallic element that exists in two main forms – diamond and graphite

carbon-14 radioactive isotope of carbon with a total of 14 neutrons and protons in its nucleus. Carbon-14 is often used in the dating of archaeological remains.

cartilage tough, elastic tissue found in the nose, ear, throat and other parts of the body

chromosome rod-shaped structure in a cell nucleus that carries the genes that determine sex and other characteristics

climate average weather of a region over a period of years

concentric circles and spheres of different sizes with the same middle point

contamination to come into contact with another thing or person that is unclean, impure or diseased and to become the same

dendrochronology study of annual growth rings in trees to date remains or determine past climatic conditions

DNA type of molecule in the form of a twisted double strand (known as a double helix) found in every cell of every living thing. It is a major component of chromosomes and carries genetic information (the information that determines an organism's characteristics).

electron negatively charged particle that orbits the nucleus of an atom

evolution development and change of plants and animals from earlier forms of life

exhume dig up a dead body for examination

fluorine testing dating method that works by measuring the fluoride ions in bone

forensic application of science in the course of a criminal investigation. Today the term also applies to the application of science to other forms of investigation, such as history or archaeology.

forensic artist any artist whose work is used to aid research or investigation into a particular subject

forgery copying, or a copy of something, that is intended to dupe others

gene basic unit consisting of a sequence of DNA that transmits characteristics from one generation to the next

ground penetration radar device that emits waves of electromagnetic radiation into the ground over an archaeological site. As these waves hit different kinds of materials underground, they are bounced back to a receiver, which interprets the signals. This can be used to form an impression of the layout of an archaeological site without having to physically excavate it.

hallucination something that someone imagines seeing or hearing that is not actually present or occurring at the time

hydraulic excavator machine used for lifting and moving large quantities of earth or soil

Ice Age period in the Earth's history when global temperatures fell and large areas of the Earth's surface were covered with ice

ice-core sampling extracting a tube of polar ice to study its chemical make-up and draw conclusions about climatic conditions in the past

ion atom or group of atoms that has acquired an electric charge by losing or gaining one or more electrons

investigation formal inquiry to find out as much information possible about something

medieval relating to the Middle Ages of Europe, a period generally considered to have occurred between the fifth and fifteenth centuries

molecule two or more atoms held together by chemical forces

motive/motivated reason for doing something

obsidian hydration dating means of dating obsidian, a type of stone. When a piece of obsidian is fractured, water from the atmosphere is attracted to its surface, causing the formation of a layer on the stone's surface known as the hydration rind that deepens with time. By measuring the depth of the hydration rind, it is possible to work out the age of the stone.

organic derived from living things

osteologist someone who specializes in studying bones

palaeontology study of life and times before history had begun to be recorded

parchment dried and treated animal hide used in earlier times for paper

particle accelerator machine used to increase the speed – and hence the energy – of the particles within an atom

physicist scientist who studies matter, energy, force and motion, and the way they relate to one another

pigment substance that is added to give something, such as paint or ink, its colour

pollen powdery substance produced by flowering plants. It is carried by the wind and insects to other plants, which it fertilizes.

radiation kind of energy that is emitted in the form of rays or waves, for example, heat, light or sound

radioactive used to describe a substance that gives off energy in the form of a stream of particles, owing to the decaying of its unstable atoms

radiocarbon dating method of dating organic remains based on their content of carbon-14

Raman microprobe spectroscopy process that can determine the chemical make-up of a substance by measuring the scattering effect caused by light rays passing through the substance

ratio proportional relationship between two different numbers or quantities

silt fine-grained mud or clay particles at the bottom of a river or lake

thermoluminescence light emitted by a substance that has been exposed to radiation in the past, such as quartz, when it is heated. Archaeologists use this technique to date rocks and pottery.

ultraviolet portion of the electromagnetic spectrum (the complete range of radiation), consisting of radiation with wavelengths beyond the violet end of the visible light spectrum

X-ray high-energy electromagnetic radiation with a wavelength that is capable of penetrating solid objects

Get into forensics

Forensics is a complex and fascinating business. Investigators may be called upon to make identifications from **DNA** fragments, take fingerprints from a scene of a crime, check photographs for fakes, examine paper fibres under an **electron** microscope, find the age of ancient bones using **radiocarbon dating**, match tyre tracks left by a getaway car or compare known dental records to the corpse of an unknown person.

Such a wide range of skills cannot be mastered by one person alone, and those involved in forensic **investigations** often perform highly specialized tasks. Ballistics experts, for example, will match projectiles with weapons and detect traces of explosives on fabric or skin. Toxicologists may be called on by a pathologist carrying out a post mortem to examine a particular organ for indications of a hard-to-detect poison.

All forensic investigators are scientific or medical professionals. In fact, the range of skills required is so broad it covers every aspect of science and medicine: physics, chemistry and biology, medicine and dentistry, **anthropology**, **archaeology** and psychology. So any reader wanting to pursue a career in this area will need some scientific qualifications.

Useful websites

Crimes and Clues: contains information about many different kinds of forensic science:
 http://www.crimeandclues.com/

Bodies of Evidence: historical mysteries and how they have been solved by science:
 http://www.channel4.com/history/microsites/B/bodies/tindex.html

BBC Archaeology: recent excavations and explanations of archaeological techniques:
 http://www.bbc.co.uk/history/archaeology/index.shtml

Further reading

Buried Worlds – Sunk!: Exploring Underwater Archaeology, Lerner Editorial Team (Lerner, 2002)

Secrets of the Dead, Hugh Miller (Channel Four Books, 2000)

You Can Make It: in Archaeology, Freya Sadarangani (Miles Kelly Publishing, 2002)

Index

Titles in the *Forensic Files* series include:

Hardback   0 431 16020 1

Hardback   0 431 16021 X

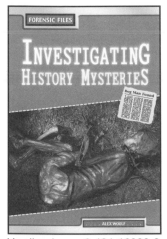

Hardback   0 431 16022 8

Hardback   0 431 16023 6

Hardback   0 431 16024 4

Hardback   0 431 16025 2

Find out about the other titles in this series on our website www.heinemann.co.uk/library